Body Activities

64 bodywork activities for therapy

Roger & Christine Day

Brook Creative Therapy

Copyright © Roger & Christine Day 2008/2011

First published in 2008 by Therapy in Romania
Revised and reprinted 2011 by Brook Creative Therapy

All rights reserved. No part of this publication may be reproduced or transmitted in any form or by any means, electronic or mechanical, including photocopy, recording or any information storage and retrieval system, without permission in writing from the publisher. Pages may be photocopied for therapeutic and training use only.

Published by:

Brook Creative Therapy, Brook Cottage, 16 Burnside, Rugby, Warwickshire CV22 6AX, UK

Details of how to order further copies can be obtained by emailing brookcreativetherapy@gmail.com

About the authors

Roger Day
Certified Transactional Analyst, Psychotherapist and Play Therapy specialist
For many years Roger has been a trainer and supervisor specialising in children and families. Now retired, he lives in Rugby, Warwickshire.

Christine Day
European Adult Teaching Certificate, Nursery Nurse Examination Board (NNEB), Diploma in Counselling, Certificate in Counselling Skills
Christine is a qualified nursery nurse. In addition to successfully raising four children, over the years she has added play and creativity specialisms to her nursery skills. Christine lives with Roger in Rugby, Warwickshire.

Books by Roger & Christine Day:

Matryoshkas in Therapy: Creative ways to use Russian dolls with clients
Creative Anger Expression
Creative Therapy in the Sand: Using sandtray with clients
Body Awareness: 64 bodywork activities for therapy (2008/2011)
Therapeutic Adventure: 64 activities for therapy outdoors (2008/2011)
Stories that Heal: 64 creative visualisations for use in therapy (2011)

Brook Creative Therapy, Brook Cottage, 16 Burnside, Rugby
CV22 6AX, UK

Acknowledgements

Body Awareness grew out of our therapeutic work, and our training of psychologists and other professionals, in the United Kingdom and in Romania. We are grateful to all those trainees and clients who facilitated the development of this project through cooperating and taking part in the various activities.

Many other people have provided input into this work.

Sharon Day modelled for us activities in creative expression through drama.

Carmen Boloş encouraged us in developing many of the dance and movement activities contained here. Her introduction to us of the Make-a-Pizza Massage has been especially helpful in our therapeutic work and training.

We are grateful to Richard Proctor and Adrian Barbu for teaching us the basics of juggling.

We acknowledge the many ideas that came from the play therapy world, notably those from Monika Jephcott and Marie Ware.

Thank you to everyone who made this project enjoyable. Apologies for any mistakes in this publication or omissions in acknowledgement.

We hope you have as much enjoyment in using these 64 activities as we had in developing them.

Roger & Christine Day

Contents

Introduction

Body needs
    Chocolate sensation
    Taste adventure
    Types of touch
    Touch tray
    Touching objects
    Smell sensations
    Safe touch
    Touch styles

Body movement
    Putting your best foot forward
    Slide whistle exercise
    Moving moods
    Ways of walking
    Life underwater
    Moving through the story
    Favourite season
    Pressing forward

Body relaxation
    Use your head
    Attention: Body at work
    Tense and relax
    Deep breaths
    Walk in the park
    Energy exchange
    Make-a-pizza massage
    Float away

Body skills
    Learning to juggle
    Rhythmic gymnastics
    Assertiveness

    Finding your strengths
    Green fingers
    Ball skills
    A positive image
    Food for thought

Body activity
    Warm-ups
    Silent-movie workouts
    Musical fitness
    Loosening up
    Making an impression
    Clay expression
    Hope for the future
    My life so far

Body awareness
    Search for treasure
    Finding your balance
    Just listen
    Body language
    Face recognition
    Breathe and sound
    Moving music
    Machinery

Body emotions
    Anger expression
    Moving through sadness
    Truck wash
    Look into my eyes
    Take care and protect yourself
    Laugh and be happy
    Stay in control
    Peace movement

Body self-care
    Self-defence
    Grounding skills

Spatial awareness
Caring for me
Saying no
Strategies for sleep
Winning formula
One good thing

Sources and references

Introduction

Body Awareness is designed as a series of creative activities for bodywork in therapy. Healthy people appreciate their bodies and enjoy their physical abilities. People who have emotional problems often do not appreciate their bodies, use negative language about themselves and their bodies, and deny their own abilities.

This book is based on the view that many emotional problems are held within the body. The book consists of 64 activities divided into eight sections, each activity relating to the body. Included is a wide range of activities, from focusing on the taste and texture of chocolate to learning self-care.

These activities can be used for any therapeutic individual or group work. They can be used in a directive or nondirective way.

Many of the activities are conducted without therapeutic comment. They enable clients to assimilate into their bodies the therapeutic changes they need. *Body Awareness* could be considered especially for clients who dissociate their feelings. These include those who are accident prone. It might also be effective with clients, adults or children, who have dyspraxia, as well as those with autistic spectrum or sensory processing difficulties.

Please note that not all the activities are suitable for every individual. The therapist knows his or her clients and can select those activities most suitable or remove those that he/she considers unsuitable or unhelpful for a particular client.

Roger & Christine Day

Body needs

Introduction

Our bodies have certain essentials for life such as food, air and warmth. In response to these external needs, we have internal regulators so that we get what we need and keep away from what is not good for us. These regulators are our senses: touch, taste, hearing, sight and smell.

Taste, for instance, helps to ensure that we do not eat something harmful to ourselves. If one of our senses is missing, such as sight, our bodies compensate by heightening other senses, such as hearing.

This series of activities focuses on senses such as smell, touch and taste. The activities are designed primarily for clients whose senses have been dulled or blocked out through trauma, abuse, abandonment issues or rejection.

Both children and adults can be affected by a dulling of the senses. Adults may forget to eat or even drink liquid. Children may engage in behaviour that causes them harm, such as repeatedly banging their heads.

In her book *The Handbook of Play Therapy* (Routledge, 1992), Linnet McMahon writes: 'Sensory work with emotionally damaged children is based on the belief that a child's senses are dulled by the many traumas that have been suffered' (page 44). She believes that through play therapy 'children can relearn to become aware of their bodies and their contact with the world around them' (page 44).

According to the theory of Sensory Processing Disorder (Kranowitz, 1998/2005), there are two kinds of affected people: sensory seekers and sensory avoiders. These exercises can assist seekers of sensations to slow down, while sensory avoiders can be encouraged to experiment around senses that are safe and can be enjoyable.

Chocolate sensation

Materials needed

Good quality chocolate that can be broken into squares. The amount will depend on the number of people taking part. Ideally, use three different flavours, each containing textured 'bits'. Examples are chocolate with crispy mint, caramel bits or orange zest. You could also consider chocolate with coffee pieces. *Safety warning: Ensure that none of the participants have peanut allergies. Alternatively, choose chocolate that is manufactured in an environment guaranteed free of contact with peanut products. If a client is allergic to chocolate, you might consider fudge as a substitute.*

Instructions

The facilitator gives out pieces of chocolate and asks the client or clients to wait until everyone is ready. The facilitator gives instructions slowly and clearly, in a similar way to a visualisation. The exercise can be repeated with the different flavours of chocolate.

It may be useful to talk through afterwards what the experience was like for each of the participants. A good ending for this exercise is to break up the remaining chocolate so that everyone gets a share to eat in a 'normal' way.

Here is a suggested way for the facilitator to talk through the exercise:

Please take a piece of the chocolate you like best and keep it until we are ready. You might need to put it on a piece of paper to stop it melting.

OK, break your piece in half and then on the count of three put one half into your mouth, but don't chew. One – two – three. Close your eyes and focus on the taste. Be aware of the sweet taste emerging as the chocolate melts. Focus on the rich, milky taste. What does it feel like in contact with your tongue, lips, cheek and teeth? Let your whole mouth be full with the sensation of the chocolate.

Now chew slowly and swallow it, staying aware of what it is like at the back of your throat.

Take the other half. Imagine you are a cat and lick it lightly. Notice the taste on your tongue. This time on the count of three put it in your mouth and immediately begin chewing slowly. One – two – three. Be aware of the texture – the softness of the chocolate, the hardness of the bits in the chocolate and the two separate tastes. Also notice the taste of the two combined. OK, you can swallow when you are ready.

Objectives

This activity can be useful for resensitising and contacting feelings and senses that have been dulled through emotional difficulties or trauma. It can also encourage slowing down to taste and feel food – useful in the case of someone with ADHD (hyperactivity) issues.

Taste adventure

Materials needed

A selection of unusual foods, cut into small pieces and kept on separate plates. Choose foods with tastes and textures that may not have been experienced by the client. This could depend on cultural backgrounds. Examples are unusual crisps, rice crackers and bread sticks broken into pieces, or corn snacks. Sweeter foods could include exotic fruit (mango, fresh fig, lychee, star fruit, etc) cut into pieces, sherbet powder and popping candy, or even old-fashioned jelly. For a more daring approach, try pieces of baby octopus or sample some raw fish such as sushi. *Safety warning: Ensure that all products used are free of peanut residue or check that participants can tolerate peanut. Avoid extremely strong or obnoxious tastes. Some foods may need to be kept refrigerated until needed.*

Instructions

Whether you are working with a group or an individual, consider yourself joining in this tasting experience. Explain to the participants that you are going to taste some unusual things. Assure clients that everything is edible and that nothing will harm them, burn their mouths or make them ill. Small pieces of a certain food are passed around without saying what they are, and at a given instruction everyone tries it together.

You as the facilitator might want to guide the experience with comments such as: 'Be aware of the taste. Now concentrate on the texture. Is if soft, crunchy, hard or strange? What is the after-taste like? Do you like what you have tasted, or hate it? Would you try it again?'

Finally, ask clients if they can identify the food.

Do this for each food. Make sure that the strongest tastes are last because otherwise they will mask gentler tastes.

Objectives

Clients of many ages like adventure, and this mild risk-taking activity is one way of fulfilling it. It can be used to help clients focus on taste and texture. Why not make this culinary 'treat' even more adventurous by tasting blindfold?

Types of touch

Materials needed

None.

Instructions

This is an exercise that involves touching each other in different ways. If you are working with a group, ensure that the group members have reached the stage where touching each other (and possibly you) is natural and safe. If you are working with an individual on his or her own, consider your own protection. It may be more appropriate to have someone else present in the room.
Suggested wording:

We're now going to explore different ways of touching each other. Without hitting, twisting, punching or kicking, we are going to go around and touch each other's arms in different ways. First imagine the other person as a friend or playmate. In what ways would you touch the other person's arm or hand?

Then:

For those of you who have been touched in this way, what's it like?

Then move on to touching as a 'mother' (consider changing this to 'caring father' if this is more appropriate for the group), 'healer' and 'antagonist/someone who doesn't like you' (Davis, 2004). In the latter case it is important to ensure that boys do not use force or violence. Be aware that children on the autistic spectrum tend to take things literally!

Objectives

This exercise helps clients to experience both touching others and being themselves touched in a safe environment. It could well be useful for clients who have been deprived of touch or who have experienced harmful or frightening forms of touch. Touching another person and being touched in this structured way could be helpful for a person (child or adult) with autistic spectrum difficulties who is not used to touch.

Touch tray

Materials needed

A large teatray and a cloth. A range of assorted household items, possibly including little ornaments, cotton wool, ribbon, velvet towelling, short lengths of lace, plastic items, nuts and bolts, spanner, etc.

Instructions

Put several assorted objects with a range of different textures on the teatray and cover everything with the cloth. Invite the client to reach under the cloth (without looking) and try to guess what the item is. If you are working with a group, get each person in turn to feel one item.
    When everyone has had several attempts at feeling the items take the cloth away. Be ready to note any comments from the participants.

Objectives

This old party game is one that delights most children and adults, too. It is useful when working with clients whose sense of touch is limited or who have lost their delicate ability to sense objects through touch as a result of autistic spectrum problems or possible abuse. It is a fun game that encourages focusing and concentrating.

Touching objects

Materials needed

A range of natural objects with interesting textures. These can include seashells, sharp and smooth stones, various kinds of bark, pinecones, driftwood, conkers, beans and seeds. Make a collection of these objects and improve your collection each time you walk in the countryside or are at the seaside.

Instructions

This is an exercise in which clients can enjoy experiencing the different textures of natural objects. Pass objects one at a time to the individual or around the group. Invite people to feel each object in various ways – with tips of fingers, in the palm of the hand, with hand wrapped around the object.

Clients who have experienced trauma or abuse sometimes find it difficult to touch objects in a way that is safe for them. They might discover the sharp parts and touch too hard or even bang the object into the palm of their hands. It is really important to show people how to touch objects so that they feel the roughness but don't hurt themselves.

Objectives

'Teaching' touch may seem a strange concept, but clients often enjoy focusing on ways of touching objects. This is a useful exercise for all clients and especially for those who have been abused or whose sense of touch has been dulled.

Smell sensations

Materials needed

A tray of 'mystery' smells, using small identical plastic containers or small squares of cloth to wrap each smell. Strong arousing smells could include lemon, chocolate, coffee, soil, rubber and vinegar. Calming scents could include banana, cinnamon, lavender, pine needles and vanilla extract.

Instructions

Get the client to identify each smell. Ensure that there is no visible evidence of the product in the container or cloth. Discuss any memories that arise as a result of the particular smell.

If you are working with a group, have a competition or a discussion about each smell.

Objectives

Smelling can heighten sensory awareness, improve attention and focus and enable better language communication. For many clients smell, unlike any other sense, can evoke memories, good and bad, that are associated with the smell. Be prepared for possible emotional responses to memories.

Safe touch

Materials needed

None.

Instructions

This exercise enables clients to practice safe ways to touch others and get the touch they need. If you are working with an individual, form a pair together. With a group, get clients to pair up. Then explore together ways of touching in an appropriate way.

With men and boys use male-type forms of touch – hand on the shoulder, a light tap on the arm, an arm wrestle, high-fives, etc.

If you are working with girls or women consider 'feminine' styles of touching – hugs, soft touching or stroking, for instance.

Objectives

This form of touching models safe touch that is acceptable for clients of both genders. Hopefully, this exercise will show that touching can be appropriate and helpful for clients.

Touch styles

Materials needed

None.

Instructions

In this exercise clients practice various kinds of touch of another person. Invite your client to try different styles, explaining that there are ways of touching that mean different things:

☐ *Ritual*
Start with an ordinary handshake. Experiment with other types such as the Roman handshake (gripping each other's right wrist) or the two-handed palm-to-palm ritual greeting. If you are working with someone with a good sense of humour, fun handshakes could include squeezing and pulling the other's hand (The Milkman), moving the other's hand in a circular motion (The Train Driver) and pumping the other hand up and down (The Road Repairer). Encourage clients to experiment with other creative handshakes.

☐ *Remedial*
Imagine the other person is feeling unwell. How would you use touch to help him or her? (Suggestions could be hand on the arm, touching the head, etc.) Then think of the person feeling unhappy (playful pat on the arm, etc) or upset (soothing, rubbing the back, etc).

☐ *Releasing feelings*
What type of touch would enable a friend to express a feeling that he or she has locked away? Think of the four basic emotions – sad, happy, scare, anger – and any other related feelings. Explore creative ways to touch the other person.

❏ *Relational*
Try different ways of touching if the other person were your very special friend. How would that be different from touching a brother or sister, a parent or a little child?

This exercise is best done without spending a lot of time discussing the different styles of touching. If discussion emerges naturally from the client, then that is another matter.

Objectives

The styles of touch exercise enables clients to explore various ways of making physical contact. It can also be quite emotional as clients realise what they may have missed in touch (or been invaded by inappropriate touch).

Body movement

Introduction

Movement is vital for life. As society increasingly advocates immobility through TV and computer-based activities, people become less able or willing to use gross motor movement on a daily basis, and this results in both physical and emotional difficulties.

On the physical side, occupational therapists have identified a condition known as Sensory Processing Disorder (SPD – formerly called Sensory Integration Dysfunction) in certain people, particularly children, including many of those with autistic spectrum difficulties. With SPD the person's senses are out of kilter with the accepted norm. One of these is what they call the Vestibular Sense, of which Balance and Movement is an important subsection.

SPD expert Carol Stock Kranowitz writes: 'Safe and appropriate physical fun strengthens our muscles and teaches us what our bodies can and can't do, how to protect ourselves, how to anticipate what's coming at us, how to make smart choices, how to make and keep friends' (Kranowitz, 2003/4, page 70).

On the emotional side, when people are able to express themselves through movement it brings a healthy emotional release. Marie Ware, a senior registered Dance Movement Therapist, points out that 'movement reflects a person's pattern of thinking and feeling. Through acknowledging and working with the person's movements, the therapist encourages exploration of new adaptive movement patterns, supporting management of accompanying emotional changes' (Ware, 2004).

These body movement exercises for clients combine the enjoyment of physical activity with emotional release through movement.

Putting your best foot forward

Materials needed

Music of the client's choice and a media player.

Instructions

Ask clients to take off their shoes – and their socks, if they want to. Encourage them to stretch and then relax their feet, followed by circling their ankles. Finally, get them to stretch their toes and relax.

Once clients have completed warm-up exercises for their feet, invite them to walk round the room on tiptoes. Encourage them to feel the muscles stretching in their feet and ankles as they walk. Invite them to appreciate the freedom they experience in being barefoot.

Play music of the client's choice – perhaps a mixture of fast, slow, loud and soft music. Invite the client to move in time with the music, concentrating just on feet.

Afterwards talk together about the sensation of focusing on feet in this activity. You might also extend this to discussing foot care. If appropriate have some foot cream available for the client to use. Discuss homecare products, standard pedicure and fish pedicure, and chiropody. Help clients to see that care for feet is part of self-care.

Objectives

This activity is designed to help clients find enjoyment in moving and stretching their feet. It increases awareness and appreciation of the feet as well as self-care. This activity encourages the use of muscles that perhaps have not been used much before. It can also be used to build confidence and self-esteem. In a group, this can be used as a skills competition with fun and laughter.

Slide whistle exercise

Materials needed

A slide whistle – available from most music stores. Sometimes small slide whistles are included in Christmas crackers. Failing all else, use a whistle with notes on it, such as a recorder or Irish whistle.

Instructions

This physical exercise can be done while sitting or standing. It is useful for all clients. It is especially useful in groups where there are one or more people in wheelchairs or who have difficulty balancing when standing.

Explain that it is an exercise involving raising and lowering the arms. When the sound goes up, clients gradually put their hands in the air. When the sound goes down they gradually put them down. This is not as easy as it sounds because the slide whistle's 'arm' goes in to produce a higher note and out to produce a lower one. Clients therefore need to listen carefully to the note rather than look at the slide whistle. By varying the speed of the slide, clients increase or slow down their movements.

A variation, especially for very active clients, is doing the same thing with legs. Get the client/s to lie on the floor. When the note goes up they put their legs in the air, and vice versa. This becomes enjoyable when the therapist leaves clients with their legs partly suspended in the air for a few seconds.

A third variation for younger clients is to do the same thing with them lying on the floor doing a sit-up when the note goes higher and lying down again when it goes down.

Objectives

This activity promotes concentration and cooperation. It emphasises the importance of relating listening to body movement. At the same time it emphasises the routine that we all need to feel good about ourselves.

Moving moods

Materials needed

None.

Instructions

Get the client/s to move around the room in an emotional way. Suggestions include:

sad
happy
angry
scared
depressed
laughing
confused
carefree
burdened
upset
excited

The facilitator changes clients to another mood by clapping or blowing a whistle. Then they instantly move their mood.
Remember that clients do not have to walk, just move. You might find that some younger clients crawl, roll, bounce, slither or run.

Objectives

This exercise encourages clients to acknowledge and experience different moods or emotions in an enjoyable, nonthreatening way. By changing body posture and movements, clients can change the way they feel and act.

Ways of walking

Materials needed

None.

Instructions

Encourage client/s to start by walking around the room at their own pace and using their own patterns.

Now invite them to walk around the room:

> hopping
> jumping
> on tiptoes
> as if string is attached to their hands
> as if string is attached to their head
> as if they have had a fabulous time
> as if they have something really to be proud of
> as if they are carrying a big bunch of helium balloons
> as if a big bunch of helium balloons is carrying them
> as if they are walking on air
> as if they are extremely happy
> as if they have made new friends

Objectives

This is an exercise for clients to feel good about the way they walk. It enables them to step into the best movements for them. Clients can perform without shame or embarrassment. It is also an enjoyable exercise with plenty of laughter and a good way to expend energy.

Life underwater

Materials needed

Pictures of sea creatures. Props to assist in the creation of sea creatures, such as streamers and coloured tissue paper. Majestic music or sea noises. (We recommend *Underwater Cave,* a CD produced by New World Music Limited.)

Instructions

Start by inviting client/s to take a look at some pictures of what is in and under the sea. Then invite them each to represent a sea creature.

If you are working with a group, invite them to get into subgroups of two or three people to represent different categories of creatures.

Each person decides on a sea creature and acts out the part to the sound of music or the sea.

If people have difficulty deciding, suggest such things as crabs, sword fish, sea slugs, dolphins, sea anemones, seaweed, whales, sharks and octopuses. They might consider being small fish to swim in and out of the coral reef. Then propose that they practice the individual movements.

Finally, add in the music/sea noises to help them create an underwater scene.

Objectives

This activity enables clients to express themselves through movement in enjoyable ways. By imagining a swimming creature or seaweed moving in the water many clients are able to engage in body movement without too much embarrassment. Through doing this they may increase their imagination and help build their confidence. When you are working with groups this activity promotes cooperation, organisation, planning and working as a team.

Moving through the story

Materials needed

Music chosen by the client and a media player.

Instructions

Explain to your client/s that in the next session you are going to invite them to show a part of their life story without words using just their bodies. Discuss with them how our bodies are affected by stress, anger, anxiety and depression and that by changing bodily movements they can move through their story to a more positive outcome. Invite them to bring music to the following session that can assist them in creating their life story.

Before they begin their life story, ask them to sit quietly and explore how they are going to depict their difficulty using movement. Rather than thinking about and planning what they will do they might be willing to use simple intuition.

When they are ready they move to the rhythm of the music they have chosen. Allow them complete freedom to express what they need to express safely and without your comments.

At the end of the movement ask them if they would like to discuss anything and, if so, what. Allow clients to de-role and get themselves grounded before the therapy session is finished.

Objectives

Moving Through the Story enables clients to express the inexpressible and unlock issues deep inside themselves. The exercise is designed to encourage clients to experience at a deep level the usual pattern of being and a different one.

If clients are able to move to a new pattern it could be seen as a form of *redecision,* a 'replacement of a self-limiting early decision by a new decision that takes account of the individual's full adult resources' (Stewart & Joines, 1987, page 333).

Favourite season

Materials needed

A selection of natural materials from the four seasons (flowers, leaves, twigs, conkers, etc). You might also consider including play scarves and simple musical instruments and A choice of CDs that have natural sounds or that evoke nature. (A favourite CD of ours for this activity is *The English Country Garden* from Dan Gibson's Solitudes.)

Instructions

The client chooses one of the four seasons (Spring, Summer, Autumn, Winter). If you are working in a group, consider dividing the clients into four subgroups to represent each season. Client/s practice specific movements to convey the season of their choice. They might show the activities of nature, people or animals during their chosen season. They may play musical instruments themselves or select an appropriate CD. Once they are ready, they 'perform' for you or for the rest of the group. If you are working as a group, see if the rest of the group can guess which season is being represented by each small group.

Objectives

This activity promotes plenty of imagination. It is an enjoyable activity in which clients can learn to move their bodies efficiently and expressively. It helps individuals to learn more about themselves and their interactions with others, increases focus and concentration and develops a healthy self-image.

Pressing forward

Materials needed

Music preferably of the client's choice. (We recommend positive songs such as *Somewhere Over the Rainbow* sung by Eva Cassidy.) A media player.

Instructions

This is a body movement activity in which clients are invited to go on an imaginary journey. They start from where they are now and continue on to where they would like to be.

The first step is to choose some music. Then clients think about how they feel in their bodies and what shapes they would like to make.

During the movement itself be respectful and give clients space for their own processes. It is important not to interrupt except for safety reasons.

When the movement is completed allow clients time to de-role and to return to the here-and-now. Clients may not want to talk about what has happened and it is important to accept this.

Objectives

This activity enables clients to look at life objectively and to move forward with hope for the future. See it as part of a positive psychology approach that can lead to real script change.

Body relaxation

Introduction

Stress is necessary for life. Without it life would be boring and drab. There would be no meaning and purpose. How clients react to stress is how they cope with life. If they go under, then stress has beaten them. But they can learn the secret of thriving under the most stressful situation.

The authors of *Stress Check* (Nicholls, et al, 1992) write: 'Relaxation is the body's natural antidote to stress. It is switching off and completely letting go – physical and mentally – and should be practiced every day by everyone, not only people who feel stressed' (page 18).

These exercises in body relaxation will hopefully be fun for the clients taking part and will also teach them the importance of relaxation in the face of life's stresses and pressures.

Warning: Effective relaxation can lower blood-sugar levels and brain-rhythm patterns. Check if clients are diabetic or epileptic and if so suggest they get approval from their doctor before they take part in these exercises.

Use your head

Materials needed

None.

Instructions

In this exercise clients explore head movements with the aim of relaxing their heads and necks. They start by sitting in comfortable chairs or lying on their backs on the floor. The next step is to relax as much as possible.

Once relaxed they raise their heads and slowly move them from left to right and back again, then right to left and back again. They continue by moving their heads up to look at the ceiling and down to look at the floor. Finally, they move their heads in a circular pattern, first one way and then the other. In each case it is important for clients to pause for a moment at the central point before continuing any of the movements. This prevents any damage to delicate muscles.

Objectives

This activity encourages concentration and promotes self-care. If done well it can lead to a feeling of elation and relaxation. If you are working with a group, success in this difficult activity can be celebrated together.

Attention: Body at work

Materials needed

None.

Instructions

Invite clients to sick back in their chairs or lie on their backs on the floor in a relaxed position. Explain using a slow, gentle voice (similar to that used for guided visualisation) that you are going to get them to concentrate on what activities are happening in their bodies.

Without getting them to feel their hearts or pulse with their hands, ask them to concentrate on their heartbeat and pulse. Then, similarly, move on to concentrating on their breathing. Invite them to be aware of their digestive processes. They might then focus on sounds they can hear within their ears, any stray dead cells moving across their field of vision away from their eyes or salvia being produced. As soon as they think of saliva they will probably start swallowing more than normal and this is a point of discussion. You might ask them to think of other processes that they can actually sense.

Once the list is exhausted, move on to imagined processes. You might get clients to sense the oxygen going into their blood, their hair growing, acid attacking their teeth, food passing into their muscles, or even their fingernails and toenails growing. Again, you might ask them to suggest further processes they can imagine happening in their bodies.

Once the relaxation is completed get clients to stand up, stretch and turn around in order to de-role.

Objectives

This exercise is useful for developing imagination and concentration skills. It can increase body and sensory awareness. For clients who are always busy, it models an enjoyable way to relax.

Tense and relax

Materials needed

None.

Instructions

Whether you are working with an individual or a group, here is a suggested form of words:

Find a comfortable place to sit back in your chair or lie down on your back on the floor, with your arms by your sides and your legs together. Think about your feet. Tense up your feet as hard as you possibly can. Hold the position for five seconds (1 – 2 – 3 – 4 – 5) and then completely relax your feet.

Now think about your legs. Tense those big muscles in your legs to make them as solid as possible. Hold for five seconds (1 – 2 – 3 – 4 – 5), and relax. Now think of your bottom. Again tense your bottom and hold it for five seconds (1 – 2 – 3 – 4 – 5), then relax. Now your legs are fully relaxed.

Focus on your stomach. Pull it in as much as you can and hold it for five seconds (1 – 2 – 3 – 4 – 5), then let it out. Now breathe in to fill your lungs with air and expand your chest as much as possible, hold your breath (1 – 2 – 3 – 4 – 5), and relax. (Pause a few seconds to let clients get their breath back.)

OK, turn your attention to your hands. Lift them up so you can see them. First, clench your fists until your knuckles show white (1 – 2 – 3 – 4 – 5), and relax them. Now stretch your fingers as far they will go (1 – 2 – 3 – 4 – 5), and relax. Now hold your hands with the palms facing each other. Stretch out your fingers so they are wide and stiff. Now, keeping your hands still, let your fingers have a fierce battle with each other (1 – 2 – 3 – 4 – 5). Let your fingers float loosely around each other. Now put your hands back on the floor.

Think of your arms, now. Tighten the muscles in your arms (1 – 2 – 3 – 4 – 5), and relax. Concentrate on your shoulders. Make your shoulders really still, hold (1 – 2 – 3 – 4 – 5), and relax.

Finally, let's move on to the neck and head. Your neck muscles have to be very strong to hold your head up and in place. Tense those big neck muscles as tight as possible, hold (1 – 2 – 3 – 4 – 5), and relax. Think about the top and sides of your head. There are lots of muscles there but they are more difficult to feel. Tense them up (1 – 2 – 3 – 4 – 5), and relax. Finally, concentrate on your face. Screw your face up, hold it (1-2-3-4-5), and relax.

Now, sit or ie there for a few seconds and be aware of what it is like to have your body fully relaxed. Close your eyes if you want to and enjoy your body being in such a relaxed state.

As the facilitator, monitor how much time clients need at the end of this exercise to appreciate fully the effect of this relaxation. The temptation is for you to rush on to the next activity but they may need a few minutes (and even a short nap) before they are ready to continue with the therapy session.

Objectives

This relaxation is a very powerful one for adults and children alike. Most experts believe that people hold problems such as anxiety and depression in their muscles. By deliberately tensing the muscles the client is accentuating any anxiety/depression. Then, by relaxing the muscles, the client is learning to 'let go' physically of the anxiety/depression.

Deep breaths

Materials needed

None.

Instructions

This is an exercise that is best done standing up. If you are working as a group, it might be useful to stand in a circle. Explain to the client/s that most people spend a lot of their time walking around with stale air in their lungs because they only use the top third of their lungs in normal everyday activity. They will have noticed the difference when they have done exercise or played sport. They get out of breath and breathe deeply until their blood has enough oxygen. When they go to sleep, their breathing pattern changes to deep, slow breathing. Deep breathing is a good way of relaxing because it gives their blood plenty of oxygen.

Ask them first to breathe in through their nose, hold their breath for a few seconds, then breathe out through the mouth. After they have tried this a few times, ask them to put one hand on the upper part of their chest and the other on the diaphragm. For those who are not sure, explain that the diaphragm is like a rubber sheet that pulls the lungs down and open when they breathe in, then contracts the lungs and pushes them up when they breathe out. The diaphragm is located at the bottom of the rib cage that they can feel with their fingers. *Caution: You might consider mentioning that the bottom of the sternum (breastbone) is quite soft and could be injured if pressed too hard.*

Once the hands are in place the client looks down and breathes deeply. The object is to ensure that the top hand stays still and the hand on the diaphragm moves in and out. This may take time and practice to achieve. Once everyone can do it, go back to the breathing exercise – in through the nose, hold, then out through the mouth. After a few times clients will hopefully feel relaxed.

Occasionally a client just can't manage this deep breathing exercise. This is not a problem. Just ask the person to lie on the floor, face down, and breathe. Quite quickly the person will learn to feel the floor of the room against his or diaphragm as the breathing deepens.

As a variation, clients can run on the spot for two minutes and count their breaths when they have stopped. Using a stop watch can give an average number of breaths per minute before exercise, when people are breathing shallowly, compared with after exercise, when people are breathing deeply.

Objectives

Deep breathing results in more oxygen being introduced into the bloodstream. This can increase a sense of wellbeing and overall relaxation and as such is recommended for everyone. Deep breathing is an excellent way to help people with hyperactivity (ADHD) to slow down. It is also useful for helping clients who are prone to panic.

Walk in the park

Materials needed

None

Instructions

Invite clients to get their bodies into a comfortable position and close their eyes if they want to. Then read the following visualisation slowly:

In your imagination you are going for a walk. Step outside. (PAUSE) It is Spring, and the sound of birds fills the air. (PAUSE)

You are in a country park. (PAUSE) There are lots of inviting footpaths through the woods and around the reservoir. (PAUSE)

Walk beside the reservoir. (PAUSE) The water is sparkling in the sunshine. (PAUSE) It looks clear and refreshing – a beautiful reflection of the sky. (PAUSE) Stop and watch the ducks and ducklings as they swim by. (PAUSE)

Listen to the water lapping gently at the banks. (PAUSE) Feel the warmth of the sun on your back. (PAUSE)

Walk along until you find a bench with the best view. (PAUSE) Sit, relax and let the everyday stresses go as you enjoy the beautiful scenery and the peace of this place. (PAUSE)

At the head of the reservoir there are two paths. Which one will you choose? (PAUSE) Will you stay close to the water's edge, with the ducks swimming busily by, the refreshing breeze and the feeling of space? (PAUSE) Or will you choose the path into the woods? It is cool in there, with dappled shade. The leaves are rustling in the breeze yet there is a feeling of stillness. (PAUSE)

Two paths. The choice is yours. (PAUSE)

Take in the scene around you. (PAUSE) Relax and enjoy all that nature has to offer you. (PAUSE)

It is time to leave now. You are welcome to come back any time. (PAUSE) The country park is always available in your imagination. (PAUSE)

When you are ready, come back into the here and now and open your eyes.

Objectives

This visualisation can help clients to find bodily relaxation and freedom from intrusive thoughts. Finding a place of peace in our minds and going there at difficult or stressful times can do wonders for our bodies as well as our minds and emotions.

Energy exchange

Materials needed

None.

Instructions

With your client (or in pairs if it is a group) place the palms of your hands close to the other person but without touching. Feel the energy or heat exchanging between the two of you. Closing eyes might help to increase the intensity of this feeling. Try moving hands closer or further apart.

Invite clients to use their imagination about the exchange of energy between the two people.

Experiment with blindfolds to see what difference it makes, if any. If you are working in a group, make a circle and feel the energy from the person on your right.

Objectives

This exercise is useful for personal development and increased sensory awareness. It is a fact that our hands are sensitive to feel the heat from someone else at a short distance. A dermatologist, for instance, can feel inflammation in the skin without actually touching it. However, this exercise is about much more than purely physical feelings. It is about imagination, creativity and drama. It includes imagining what the other person can give through energy exchange to help his or her partner. For a group it encourages teambuilding and group formation.

Make-a-pizza massage

Materials needed

None, but plenty of imagination is useful.

Instructions

The idea of this massage exercise is to make an imaginary pizza gently on your client's back, putting on some of your own and his/her favourite toppings. Then, depending on your approach to therapy, it may be appropriate for your client to do the same for you.

If you are working with a group, the ideal way is to stand in a circle, including you as the facilitator, turn to the right and make a pizza on the back of the person in front of you. *Warning: This exercise needs cooperation from all group members. You might need to establish a contract of gentleness before you start or else things could get out of hand and people could end up with being karate chopped!*

Here are some suggested words for guiding this exercise:

Let's make a pizza on each other's backs. First spread some flour on the surface. (PAUSE) Knead the dough. (PAUSE) Then smooth it out into a circle to make a base. Spread on the tomato paste. Now for the toppings. First put some slices of ham on. (PAUSE) Dot the olives all over the pizza. (PAUSE) Sprinkle with corn. (PAUSE) Scatter mushrooms here and there. (PAUSE) Add slices of tomato. (PAUSE) Sprinkle on the cheese. (PAUSE) Put it in the oven. (PAUSE)

It's ready. Take it out of the oven. (PAUSE) Slice it. (PAUSE) Now eat it. (PAUSE)

You could explain how to do each movement or you could leave it up to the client/s creativity.

Finally, ask clients how they are feeling after that exercise.

Objectives

Pizza Massage is a gentle and healing form of touch that for most clients seems safe. Be aware, though, that many survivors of sexual abuse may find it too intrusive and may need alternative forms of touch. When you are working with a group, it is a way of group relaxation. It shows effective loving and caring to others in a way that most clients can accept.

Float away

Materials needed

Gentle music (possibly of the client's choice) and a media player.

Instructions

Invite clients to relax in their chair or sit or lie on the floor, making sure there is plenty of room for them to move. They can close their eyes or leave them open. As the music plays, invite them to imagine they are floating, moving around, staying in time to the music. It is best if they stay in the chair or on the floor. If you are working with a group, it is essential that group members don't touch or crash into each other.

A variation could be to suggest that clients move around on their feet as if they were floating in the air or on water. Again, if you are working with a group it is important that they respect each other's space.

Objectives

This exercise enhances creativity, relaxation and body awareness. It is ideal for clients with ADHD (hyperactivity) or coordination difficulties (dyspraxia) because they need to slow down and move in time to the music. The activity promotes muscle control and helps coordination and dramatic expression.

Body skills

Introduction

Many people enjoy a challenge, and clients are no exception. Even those who don't like sport will get enthusiastic about something that is new, different and enjoyable, such as many of these activities

Children who take part in organised sport, such as soccer, are often under huge pressure to achieve. When they fail to achieve they feel bad about themselves, or are criticised by others, which can lead to low self-esteem in later life. Many adult clients present with these feelings of failure. This section of activities under the title *Body Skills* is about tackling challenging activities in an enjoyable way and building confidence and self-esteem as a result. Clients can celebrate each step towards achieving their goal.

Sports psychologists refer to 'peak performance' in sport, which means playing at the very best of one's ability, not merely 'trying hard' (which is a good recipe for failure). Characteristics of peak performance are:

a. Relaxed. Clients don't need to be 'psyched up' to do their best. They need to feel relaxed, with an undercurrent of energy.
b. Confident. They expect to succeed. They trust in their own instinct and intuition.
c. Focus. Clients need to be totally absorbed in the moment, with no sense of time.
d. Effortless. Peak performance means their movements are smooth, even graceful, with the mind and body in perfect harmony.
e. Automatic. Clients achieve good results in body skills when apparently no conscious thoughts or emotions are involved.
f. In control. They feel in control of what they are doing, so that what they think will happen actually does happen.
g. Enjoyment. A sense of enjoyment and interest is essential.

If you as the facilitator are willing to work with clients in understanding the activities and helping them to succeed even in a small way, it will be a major step forward therapeutically.

Learning to juggle

Materials needed

Three small juggling balls per person. These can be bought in hobby shops or specialist juggling stores. They need to be equal in size and weight, preferably filled with beans to make them easier to catch.

As part of the activity with clients, balls can be made by attaching a funnel on to the open end of a good quality balloon and filling it with rice or lentils. The balloon needs to be thoroughly stretched first (perhaps blown up a couple of times) and the contents need to be packed well into the balloon until a decent size is achieved. The end and neck of the balloon is cut off and another balloon of the same colour is stretched over the first balloon to cover the hole. The end and neck are again cut off. When the outside balloon starts to wear out, simply add another balloon.

Alternatively, for quick success, use three chiffon scarves (sometimes available in charity shops). Other forms of juggling can be tried, including devil sticks or diablo.

Instructions

The key to success in juggling is practice and a regular rhythm. Keeping the elbows in can also help with aiming correctly.

The idea is to start with only one ball. The person stands facing a wall so that he or she throws the ball close to and not away from the body. The ball is thrown in an arc shape from one hand to the other. The top of the arc needs to be level with the person's head. The person throws it slowly and rhythmically from one hand to the other and back until he or she can do it with eyes closed.

The next step is to take a ball in each hand. The client throws the ball with the left hand into the same arc as before. As the ball begins to fall, he/she throws the other ball in a slightly smaller arc so that it will go underneath the first one.

After catching the first ball, the client throws it again and continues. Again, get the person to practise until this stage can be done with eyes closed. *Remind the person to avoid passing a ball across from one hand to another. This is the biggest temptation when starting to juggle.*

The final stage is to use three balls. Although juggling looks like there are three balls in the air, this is an illusion. There is always only one ball in the air. The two others are in the left and right hands. The person starts with a ball in the right hand and two in the left hand. The person then throws one ball from the left hand as before. When it has nearly reached the right hand, he/she throws the right ball into the air and catches the ball that is coming down. The ball from the right hand arcs towards the left hand. Again, the client throws the ball in that hand just before catching the one coming down.

This is not an easy task and can take many hours of frustrating practice to accomplish.

Objectives

Learning to Juggle, even at the beginning stages, helps build clients' confidence and the thought: 'I can succeed!' The exercise encourages persistence and determination. If focuses the attention and is therefore good for clients with ADHD (hyperactivity) or concentration problems. It is a great assistance to improving coordination. People on the autistic spectrum can become highly competent by focusing on one specific skill that is seen by others as socially acceptable.

The facilitator can aid the difficult process of learning this skill with plenty of encouragement at each stage of achievement.

Rhythmic gymnastics

Materials needed

Music of the client's choice and a media player. Coloured ribbons and crepe paper streamers long enough to swirl around.

Instructions

Rhythmic gymnastics can be a beautiful and powerful way to express feelings. (See cover picture for an example.)

Ask your clients to select music to suit the feelings they will be expressing in this movement. Invite them to choose the streamers or ribbons they will be using. Some clients will want to use several streamers; others may prefer just one.

Many clients find it more liberating to take off their shoes and even their socks for this activity.

As the music starts encourage clients to express themselves through their bodies, using the streamers and while moving around the room. The freedom to express their feelings completely could be scary for clients and they may need to start very gently.

During the activity watch carefully clients' faces and body postures to see how they are coping and when they are ready to stop. Afterwards, discuss the activity in as much detail as the client wants and needs.

Objectives

This activity will hopefully build clients' confidence and enable them to express through their bodies what they struggle to express in words. The freedom experienced by this activity may be seen as a metaphor for freedom from the difficulties they have faced in life that brought them to therapy in the first place.

Assertiveness

Materials needed

None.

Instructions

Discuss with clients the need to stand up for themselves without becoming aggressive or ending up being the victim. Explore with clients the importance of getting their needs met and how this can be achieved. Then role-play situations where assertiveness skills are needed. Here are some examples:

At work
A colleague marches into your office and demands angrily: 'Who's been using my mug?' How do you respond? What can you do to diffuse the situation?

At home
Your family members leave things everywhere. They never help with any jobs around the house. They expect you to do everything. How will you deal with this? Will you continue to be passive, or will you stand up for yourself and delegate tasks?

Socially
At the gym, everyone seems to get on the equipment before you. It is as if you are invisible. Do you let them ignore you, or do you stand your ground in order to get your turn?

School/College
At break times the same person always seems to laugh when you walk by and make rude comments about your trainers. Do you pretend you don't hear the comments, or do you tell someone in authority?

Objectives

This exercise can be life-changing for clients as they come to realise that they have rights, too. It will hopefully help them to value themselves and manage life more successfully. Learning assertiveness skills can boost a client's confidence and self-esteem.

Finding your strengths

Materials needed

Plastic sheet, brushes, poster paint, paper and pots of water.

Instructions

Spend time with clients exploring their strengths, abilities, skills and attributes. Get them to paint a picture of their strengths – an abstract impression or something tangible. Assure clients that there is no standard to attain to. Their painting is acceptable to the therapist.

While clients are working watch their facial expressions, listen to their breathing and take not of any comments they might make. If they need encouragement tell them the good points you have observed in them.

When the painting is finished, encourage clients to tell you about the painting and how it could give them confidence.

Objectives

The aim of this exercise is to make space for clients to acknowledge their strengths, abilities, skills and attributes and to bring them to the fore by putting them on paper. This exercise could help to build confidence and self-esteem.

Green fingers

Materials needed

Plants that you can take cuttings from, compost, pots, dibber, strong scissors, plastic sheet to protect the floor.

Instructions

Have available a selection of plants and talk about them. What are they like? Are they attractive? Colourful? Evergreen? Are they flowering plants or do they just produce foliage?

How do the plants protect themselves? Do they need a lot of care or do they thrive on neglect?

Invite clients to choose which one/s to take cuttings from. Explore in what ways the chosen plant/s are like the client.

Facilitate clients in preparing the cutting/s and planting them in pots. Don't do it for them. This is their skill, not yours.

Talk about nurturing, the needs of the cutting for growth and life. Does the cutting need sun or shade? How much water does it need, and how often? When will it need feeding and what plant food will the client use?

Explore with clients how the cuttings might feel away from the main plant. Talk about roots reaching down into the soil, leaves growing up towards the warmth of the sunlight.

Encourage clients to take their cuttings home and care for them. Invite clients to report regularly on the progress of the cuttings as their own therapy progresses.

Objectives

This exercise involves giving clients something to nurture. It encourages them to take care of themselves and gives them permission and responsibility to care for the plant as well as for themselves.

Ball skills

Materials needed

Three small balls of the same size. Possibly raw eggs.

Instructions

Ball skills do not seem like therapy at all, yet they have their value. Most clients will gladly join in. Any activity involving catching a ball and throwing it accurately will do for this activity. We have included below some of our favourite ball activities, described for working in a group, though the list is endless. If you are working with an individual, you can adapt the activity appropriately.

Throwing and catching
Simple throwing and catching exercises help clients to gain competence and speed. Stand in a circle and throw the ball to someone, who then throws it to someone else, and so on across the circle. A useful adaptation is for the person with the ball to throw it saying his or her own name. Later, when the names are well known, throwers can say the name of the person they are throwing to. An adaptation is for everyone to catch the ball in the usual way and then to throw it from behind their back.

Ball patterns
Stand in a circle and throw the ball to someone. That person then throws it to a different person and so on until everyone has a turn. The last person throws it back to the first person. Now you have a pattern. Repeat the pattern several times until everyone is remembering the pattern and feeling confident. Then introduce a second ball into the same pattern. To make it more difficult speed up the throwing or add a third ball.

Objectives

Developing ball skills such as catching and passing a ball can help a client feel confident in many situations. Underachieving clients who believe they are no good at anything can get good results through these activities. They are great for building confidence, improving hand-eye coordination and increasing gross motor skills.

A positive image

Materials needed

Plastic sheet, glass paints, brushes, pot of water. Mirror provided by the client.

Instructions

Ask clients to bring a mirror to the session to use for a painting exercise. Ideally, it will be a mirror that they will use regularly.

Talk with your clients about some positive messages they can say about themselves. When clients have decided on a chosen affirmation that fits for them, discuss together where on the mirror the message should go: Top, bottom, either side or right across the middle.

It may be useful to draft out on paper the message and any decorations they plan to use. Then invite the client to use the paints to create and decorate their mirror with a positive message.

When the paint has dried thoroughly (possibly the following week), clients take the mirror home and use it as a daily reminder of their own positive affirmation.

Objectives

A Positive Image can be used to help clients gain confidence in themselves and their abilities. The daily reminder when they look in the mirror can help to reinforce the positive work you are doing in the therapy room.

Food for thought

Materials needed

Selection of fruit and possibly fruit juice. Chopping board. Sharp knife. Peeler. A large bowl and two small bowls and spoons. Kitchen roll and a plastic sheet.

Instructions

Discuss with clients the importance of food and of regular eating even when they don't feel like it.

Invite them to start preparing a fruit salad based on the fruit you have provided. Talk about self-care and nutrition as they prepare the fruit. While they are peeling skins or removing cores discuss the therapeutic process and how people may need to let go of negative thinking, feeling and behaviour. Consider how the colours and textures of the prepared fruit complement each other. Discuss how clients can relate to others, thus enriching their own lives.

Once the fruit salad is ready, invite clients to share it if they would like. Be prepared to eat some of the fruit salad yourself, appreciating the clients skills.

Objectives

Food for Thought is a practical activity in self-care and the associated skills of preparing and presenting food. It is ideal for clients whose interest in food has declined through depression or anxiety. It encourages sharing, cooperation and healthy connections.

Body activity

Introduction

It is an established medical fact that physical activity not only benefits the body but increases emotional and psychological well-being.

Through keeping their bodies fit, clients can reduce tendencies towards anxiety and depression. Regular exercise can help them to deal effectively with stress and find safe, constructive ways of letting out their build-up of anger.

Exercise reduces body fat, building and maintaining healthy bones, joints and muscles. Being stronger and fitter will almost certainly increase a client's confidence and self-esteem.

Experts recommend that everyone exercises enough to be out of breath at least two or three times a week. Hopefully, the activities in this section are interesting enough to put body activity high on the client's agenda during the sessions with you and for their rest of his life.

Warning: Ensure that clients taking part in these exercises (and the facilitator, too) have warmed up all their muscles first with slower exercises. Failure to do this could result in pulled muscles, whatever the age of the participant.

Warm-ups

Materials needed

None

Instructions

Warm-ups should be done before any other energetic physical activities. They will be good for you as the facilitator, too! Start with gentle stretches and twists, touching toes, stretching backwards as far as possible, perhaps some star-jumps, sit-ups and press-ups. Increase the difficulty as the client/s become loosened up. Be willing to introduce exercises suggested by clients.

Try introducing some elements of enjoyment yourself. A favourite of ours is running on the spot.

Warm-ups should be followed by a few seconds of rest for everyone to get their breath back. Rushing into another exercise can be discouraging, especially for clients who are not used to exercise.

Objectives

Warm-ups can be plenty of fun if done properly. They are an excellent way of starting each session with young people, even if the other activities are not physical ones. Warm-ups can help to deal with any build-up of anger. The endorphins released will hopefully leave clients feeling good about themselves.

Silent-movie workouts

Materials needed

A metronome, available from music shops, or a noisy clock (such as an old-fashioned alarm clock). Failing all else, you as the facilitator can clap a rhythm.

Instructions

Set the metronome to about 60 beats a minute (the musical speed known in Italian as Andante). After doing some warm-ups, the idea is to do exercises to the beat of the metronome. Many actions can be done in this regular way. They include star-jumps, bunny-hops (alternating with feet between hands and feet outside hands), press-ups and sit-ups. As clients get used to the rhythm and pattern they will probably be amused to think of their jerky movements as being like taking part in a very old silent movie.

As an alternative try speeding up and then slowing down the pace.

Warning: This exercise, because of its repetitive nature, could cause injury. Watch to make sure no one is over-exerting him/herself.

Objectives

The consistent, regular movements of *Silent-movie Workouts* correlate approximately with a person's heartbeat, so clients will hopefully feel coordinated. People on the autistic spectrum will enjoy the consistency while those with hyperactivity will hopefully learn to pattern their actions in time with the metronome. This activity is also an enjoyable way to help with group formation.

Musical fitness

Materials needed

A track of music, preferably with a fast, but clear, beat. A media player.

Instructions

The idea of this activity is for client and therapist to do workouts together, exactly in time to the music. The kind of exercises you choose is less important than ensuring that the client and you keep in time with the music. If you as the facilitator are good at improvising, simply lead an exercise and change to the next one when there is a suitable change in the music. You may need to call 'Change' or say the kind of exercise above the sound of the music. If you are not as good at improvising, write a list of the exercises you plan to do, then keep it in front of you on the table or the floor so that you can continue to lead the exercises without having to fumble through paper.

If you as the facilitator are musically trained and/or experienced, you might like to experiment with different time signatures: following exercises at the rate of three, four or six beats to a bar. For clients who like rock music, see if they can do eight actions for the eight beats to a bar.

As a variation, get clients to lead the exercises while you follow.

Objectives

Musical fitness is a popular way to keep fit. It is also a way of encouraging clients to listen, focus and cooperate. By varying the tempo of the music and/or the rate of exercise you can help clients to develop more effective listening skills.

Loosening up

Materials needed

None. Music may help to make this activity even more enjoyable. If so, remember a media player.

Instructions

This activity will enable clients to become relaxed and ready to enjoy life. Explain to clients you work with that, like a car, our bodies need to have a good tune-up now and again to work efficiently. Start by shaking arms and shoulders to get all the tension out of them. Do this for at least 30 seconds. While continuing to do this, concentrate on loosening up the hands (again, for at least 30 seconds). Then, still loosening the arms and shoulders, start moving the head up and down, round and round. Make sure that clients don't do this too vigorously or else they might end up with a pulled muscle in their neck, the opposite to what they are attempting to achieve.

While keeping up the same movements, focus on the hips. The idea here is to move the hips round and round as if using a hoola-hoop or doing the Twist. Now focus on the knees, bending and straightening them slightly, alternating them if possible. Again, be careful not to hurt the knees by doing this too vigorously. Finally, concentrate on the feet, flexing them, standing on tiptoes and back again. Alternate the feet, at the same time keeping everything moving.

Continue the relaxing throughout the body for another minute before stopping. Then, stretch up as high as possible, fingertips pointing upwards and high on tiptoes. Then stretch the arms sideways. Finally, stretch up again, yawn, and then let out a very big sigh. Tell clients that they are now loosened up and ready for action!

For added enjoyment, especially with younger clients, get them to loosen up their tongue. After the body is fully relaxed, get them to stick out their tongues while looking down towards the floor. Keeping tongue reasonably still, move head sideways, at the same time making an ahhhh sound. The result is usually hilarious and is almost guaranteed to relax everyone with laughter. *Caution: Ensure that vulnerable clients do not end up biting their tongues!*

Objectives

Relaxation is an important way of dealing with problems of anxiety, panic, depression and stress. Doing it in a fun way like this makes relaxation a joy and something to look forward to. Most clients will find this exercise helpful. Even those with hyperactivity will hopefully let out their energy in the activity and end up reasonably relaxed.

Making an impression

Materials needed

Plastic sheet, roll of wallpaper lining or big sheets of paper, paints, brushes, water, pots, kitchen roll, hand wipes.

Instructions

Invite clients to put paint on their hands and then make colourful handprints on the paper. Talk with clients about their unique finger and hand prints. When they make their mark on the paper it says: 'I am important. I am here.'

Get clients to experiment in painting parts of their hands in different colours. If clients are adventurous ask them to squidge the paint in their hands and to feel its texture.

Some clients may be interested in putting paint on their feet and feel the sensation of paint between their toes. Clients can walk on the paper. The therapist needs to ensure that clients don't slip when doing this.

Objectives

This exercise could be useful for clients who have experienced trauma or abuse and as result have shut down their feelings. As they work together the therapist can encourage the client to take a risk.

It may take several sessions to accomplish this task as clients look at their thoughts and feelings about it. It is important that clients move step by step at their own pace towards achieving the goal.

Clay expression

Materials needed

Plastic sheet. Potter's clay (obtainable in bulk through the internet). An alternative is playdough. Clay tools. Wooden board. Hand wipes.

Instructions

Discuss with clients how they could express themselves using clay. Assure them that they don't have to produce anything beautiful. It is only a means of expressing themselves, not for producing a work of art. Talk together about what clients want to achieve through this exercise.

It could be that spending time kneading and squeezing the clay is in itself a therapeutic experience.

Facilitate clients in engaging with the clay in whatever they want. This could include expressing anger by banging the clay and shouting. It could involve creating something (such as hope or safety) that the client needs right now. It could also be a shape or a figure that the client uses to symbolise where they are at in their therapeutic journey.

After clients have finished, ask them what they want to do with the clay. They might want to throw it away, keep it to remind them about the activity or put it back into the stock of clay for someone else to use.

Objectives

Clay Expression gives clients the opportunity to express themselves and move on in life, leaving difficulties behind or taking positive changes forward as they work the clay.

Hope for the future

Materials needed

None.

Instructions

Talk with clients about their life right now and what they hope for in the future. Ask them to sculpt a pose showing how their life is now. Then ask them to sculpt a pose of how they hope their life will be in the future. The poses are done in silence with you as the therapist being the observer. If clients are in agreement you can take a photograph of both the poses and look at them together.

Spend time talking about clients' hope for the future as portrayed through the second pose. Look together at practical steps clients can take to achieve their hopes and dreams.

Objectives

This exercise enables clients to look at their life from a different perspective and to project their hopes forward into a positive future. When they create their positive dream using their body it helps to bring the dream into reality. As E Y Harburg wrote in *Somewhere Over the Rainbow:*

'The dreams that you dare to dream
Really do come true.'

My life so far

Materials needed

None.

Instructions

Discuss with clients their life up to the present. Encourage them to look at good, positive things as well as negatives. Once these have been discussed invite clients to do a dance or series of moves depicting their life so far.
    It is best to watch in silence as clients move around the therapy room. Be sensitive to their needs, watching their face for any sign of distress. Ensure that the moves they make finish on a positive note. If this doesn't happen, remind them that through all the ups and downs of life they have survived. This shows that they have strength within them to become a winner.
    When the dance/movement finishes invite the client to reflect on what has happened and their thoughts and feelings about it. Do not interpret; allow clients to come to their own conclusions about the movement.

Objectives

This activity gives clients time to reflect on their lives and to highlight the positives. When they use their bodies to dance or move in this thoughtful way, it enables them to see things differently, giving them strength to carry on.

Body awareness

Introduction

Awareness of the body comes naturally to most of us. For clients who have been abused or who have autistic or sensory difficulties, however, activities to encourage greater body awareness can prove helpful. Being aware of the body can also help with control of the symptoms of anxiety and panic.

Our bodies have basic needs such as for food, water, air and warmth. Psychiatrist Eric Berne points out that we as humans also have three kinds of 'hungers' – stimulus/sensation hunger, recognition hunger and structure hunger (Berne, 1972/75). Tony White later added to the list 'attachment hunger' (White, 1997). We crave sensation and stimulation; we need recognition from and interaction with other people; we long to be part of a structured group; and we desperately need attachment first to a primary carer and then to others throughout life. Clients who have poor body awareness may be missing out on satisfying their hungers in these areas.

Such clients are said to be discounting at stimulus level (see Stewart & Joines, 1987, pages 181-7). They may be hungry or thirsty but don't seem to notice. They may not acknowledge aches and discomfort in their body until treatment is radical because they have left it so long.

Clients with sweaty hands, rapid breathing or heart palpitations may not be able to relate these symptoms to the scare they originally experienced. Their anxiety and panic may be seen by others as a problem of timidity or nervousness. Such clients are discounting the original stimulus that is resulting in the current symptoms.

The body awareness activities are enjoyable and also useful for stimulating awareness of clients' bodies that may been lost months or years earlier.

Search for treasure

Materials needed

Post-It notes in various colours, felt-tip pens.

Instructions

Ask your clients to relax and sit comfortably, being aware of the quietness in the room.

Tell them that in their imagination they are going on a treasure hunt. Encourage clients to be aware in their bodies of treasures they already have. Such treasures could include their own positive qualities, skills and achievements. It could also involve other people and the treasure those people bring to clients' lives.

Leave plenty of space for clients to be aware about their treasure, perhaps assisted by you through a guided visualisation.

When they are ready, invite them to show their various treasures through dramatic expression, using their bodies rather than simply talking.

The final stage is to help clients to value their treasures. Invite them to write down aspects of their treasure on coloured Post-It notes. They can then take these home and stick them on the fridge or other prominent places as a daily reminder of the treasure they already have.

Objectives

This exercise focuses on the positives in clients' lives and how they can express those treasures nonverbally through their bodies. Often clients in therapy get stuck in the 'problems'. They also need some positive treasure to help them through the difficult times.

Finding your balance

Materials needed

Any kind of rope or ribbon – at least six metres long. Scarves for blindfolds. Possibly music and media player.

Instructions

As the facilitator, lay out the rope/ribbon in a zigzag pattern around the room. Suggest that clients remove shoes (and socks, if the surface is suitable). Help clients to wear a blindfold. They put a foot on each side of the rope, feeling the rope between their feet. They then walk along the rope to the end. If it is suitable and safe, the same activity can be done walking backwards

A second activity involves walking on the rope, balancing like a tightrope walker. Again, this can be done backwards.

Alternatively, do these activities to music, moving in time to the music.

An alternative for a group is for each client to walk along the rope as in the two activities above and, when one client meets another, move past the other person without stepping off the rope.

Objectives

Finding Your Balance is an ideal activity for bilateral coordination, balance and posture. It is also helpful for stimulation through the feet and toes. Clients may like to make their own patterns with the rope. This will stimulate their imagination. This activity is good for clients who are uncoordinated or have dyspraxia.

Just listen

Materials needed

None.

Instructions

Whether you are working with an individual or a group, the idea is the same. Clients sit with eyes closed. They are invited to keep completely silent and 'just listen'. They make a mental note of all the sounds they hear over a given period of time, depending on their ability to concentrate.

At the end of the period, all sounds are named. In a group, people can take it in turns to name the sounds. Identify whether the sounds are a long way off, near or actually within the person's body.

A variation is to open a window and focus on the sounds coming from outside. At the end of a set period (which may be shorter if it is cold), clients identify sounds that come only from outside.

Objectives

Just Listen assists clients in concentration and sensory awareness. Sitting quietly can help them to become self-aware, which can assist with resensitising after trauma or abuse. Tuning-in with their ears can be a fascinating way of understanding how their bodies tune-in or tune-out to sensory stimulii around. Concentrating and sitting still for short periods will also assist in coping better in daily life.

Body language

Materials needed

Pictures of people from various magazines.

Instructions

Look with clients in magazines at various pictures of people with and decide what each person is thinking or feeling.

It is important for clients to realise that body language can sometimes be confusing. For instance, a man might be folding his arms because he is cold or because the photographer thought that was the best way to pose. The person with his hand beside his mouth could indicate that he is telling a lie and is using his hand like a small child to try to stop himself lying. It could also be that he is rubbing an itch on the side of his face!

Objectives

Understanding body language in others can enable clients to understand their own body language and perhaps why people react to them in the way they do. Learning the way others are feeling and thinking can help clients with poor social awareness to respond in ways that are more appropriate to the other person's mood.

Face recognition

Materials needed

Pictures of faces from various magazines, each one clearly showing an emotion.

Instructions

This exercise is primarily about understanding how and why people recognise emotions on other people's faces. It came out of our separate work with young people on the autistic spectrum, people who have difficulty recognising and understanding other people's facial expressions. Explain to clients that you are going to look together at various pictures of faces and say what the expression means and why you understand that a particular facial expression means a specific emotion. This includes clues from the position of the mouth and eyebrows, creases on the face, etc.

One way to approach this exercise is to explain that people with autistic spectrum difficulties usually have problems reading emotions on faces. One person in 50 is also thought to have elements of a difficulty called face blindness (prosopagnosia), which means that they have problems recognising a family member or a neighbour and the emotions they are showing. Ask clients to work out how they would explain to such people what to look for on a person's face. For instance, eyebrows down near the eyes and mouth corners turned down could be an indication of someone being angry.

If you have a group with one or more clients on the autistic spectrum, get the other group members to explain to those individuals what to look for on a face when a person is happy, angry, scared, sad, etc. See if those on the autistic spectrum have grasped the concept from what the other group members have told them.

If you want more background information on this fascinating subject read chapter 6 of *Blink* (Gladwell, 2006) on the comprehensive face-mapping work of Silvan Tomkins and Paul Ekman.

Objectives

Clients will probably enjoy working out what exactly it is on the face of someone that results in people assuming that person is feeling a particular emotion. Assisting others in a group context can help clients with awareness of their own bodies and emotional responses.

Breathe and sound

Materials needed

None.

Instructions

Warning: Before starting this exercise make sure that your client does not have asthma or other breathing difficulties. The same applies when working with a group.

This is a facilitator-led exercise involving various ways of breathing to promote body awareness. Start by getting clients to breathe normally. If you are working with a group, get them to sit in a circle first. Then suggest different ways of breathing:

Loudly
Silently
Fast
Slow
Deep
Shallow

Then get clients to breathe noisily. Younger clients might consider noises such as those made by a tiger, a dragon, a horse, a hummingbird, a snake and a crocodile. Encourage them to be aware of where in their head and throat the noise is coming from.

For a variation get clients to take a very deep breath and see how long they can breathe out for. The facilitator and the rest of the group count to measure the breath. Be careful, however, that an enthusiastic client doesn't overdo it and end up fainting.

Objectives

This exercise can enable clients to become aware of their own breathing and how they can use their bodies to control it. This can help in dealing with anger and coping with anxiety and panic. Clients with hyperactivity (ADHD) could find this a calming exercise.

Moving music

Materials needed

Source of music to suit your clients' needs. Media player. You could ask clients to bring their own music or choose music for them. In the case of active young people we suggest the theme music from *Star Wars*. Another possibility is *Everybody is Kung Foo Fighting,* by Carl Douglas. If you go to YouTube you can find a version of this song with a compilation of light-sabre action from the *Star Wars* movies. You might consider showing the video with the music.

Instructions

Get clients to listen to the music all the way through. Then talk about what feelings they could express through their bodies when the music is played a second time. If you have a children's group, ensure that you have a safety contract about not touching each other.

Then play the music again, allowing clients to express feelings through their bodies inspired by the music. Feelings could include sadness, scare, anger or joy. The music could inspire a movement to tell the client's story. It could show the client's aspirations and dreams. Encourage clients to experience the movement to the music focusing on their hands, then in turn their arms, shoulders, trunk, legs and feet.

If you are working with young people, they might want to use light-sabre action to the sci-fi music, making the noises with their mouths over top of the music. Be prepared for some lively action.

Objectives

The activity *Moving Music* is primarily about enjoyment, exploring movement with the body and expressing feelings safely and in a creative way. It will help clients to be aware of using their muscles in an expressive way. Be prepared to play the music two or three times.

Machinery

Materials needed

None.

Instructions

If you are working with one client, adapt the instructions below for just the two of you taking part.

Explain to the group that they are going to make a noisy machine using their bodies. Decide together the first type of machine you are going to make. Suggestions include a laughter machine, a music machine, an atmosphere purifying machine and an anti-global warming machine. Get clients to show movements and sounds they can make with their bodies that fit in with the type of machine being created. Get clients to arrange themselves in the room so that the machine fits together. Then someone switches on the machine and the noisy movement begins.

Afterwards sit down and talk about how participants experienced the machine in their bodies.

Possibly develop several different machines and follow the same procedure.

Objectives

This exercise focuses on body awareness and expression. In the case of groups it also includes cooperation and teambuilding. Young people will love expressing their feelings fully with plenty of grinding, shunting and small explosions from the mouth to accompany the movements.

Body emotions

Introduction

It is an established fact that enjoyment and laughter actually reduce the amount of stress hormones in the body. Letting go of problems and just laughing – for the fun of it – is good for a person's heart. The same can be said of expressing anger and sadness.

Exercises of any kind increase endorphin levels and this has an impact on levels of happiness and well-being. When clients are happy and in a good frame of mind, they can think more clearly, are better able to face reality and can find easier solutions to their problems.

Experts point out that being emotionally aware and expressing emotions through activities can help clients in several ways:

- ❐ Make effective decisions.
- ❐ Become more aware of others' needs and wants.
- ❐ Find and own their individual preferences.

Emotional awareness is vital for clients to cope and find stability in an ever-changing world.

Anger expression

Materials needed

Several cushions/pillows, scrap paper.

Instructions

Talk with clients about anger. When they feel angry, where in the body do they feel it? What do they say? What do they do? What are they thinking?

Discuss safe anger expression. Assure clients that anger is OK. Expressing anger inappropriately is not useful and can be harmful to others and to property.

Invite clients to try out some techniques for safe anger expression.

Consider starting with cushions. Place a cushion on the floor and get clients to punch lightly, feeling the floor through the cushion. This will help clients realise the importance of safety with all anger work. Add more cushions until they can't feel the floor when they punch the top cushion. Depending on the quality of cushions and the strength of clients, the pile may be quite high and it may be necessary to hold each side while they engage in the anger expression. Make sure you as the therapist keep your hands well out of the way. Then encourage clients to let anger out fully, punching hard and perhaps speaking words or making noises at the same time. Clients continue until they are exhausted or their built-up anger has subsided.

Another anger expression involves scrap paper. Demonstrate how tearing a piece of paper gently is not anger expression. Tearing with energy and force, possibly with words or other noise as they do so, enables clients to express anger in a positive way. When they have finished they can pick up all the pieces of paper and use some force to throw them into the recycling bin.

Objectives

In the UK and other Western societies anger expression is frowned upon. These exercises help clients to understand their anger and to find safe, appropriate ways to express their legitimate anger in ways that do not go against the cultural norms.

Moving through sadness

Materials needed

None.

Instructions

Discuss with clients about sadness and its significance. Consider the stages of grief. For example, Kübler-Ross (1969) has five stages: denial; anger; bargaining; despair; acceptance.
When someone we know dies we often have four stages of mourning:

- ❐ Accept the reality of the loss
- ❐ Work through the pain of grief
- ❐ Adjust to an environment in which the deceased is missing
- ❐ Emotionally relocate the deceased and move on in life

Once the stages are clear, explore with clients which stage they are at. Then invite them to use movement or dance to express aspects of their own sadness, grief, loss and mourning. If they are willing they can also show the stage of moving through to acceptance of the loss.
At the end discuss with clients what the experience was like for them. It is not necessary to analyse every part of the movement, just what clients want to discuss.

Objectives

Moving Through Sadness helps clients to acknowledge their feelings of loss and sadness and to express those feelings with their body. The activity can help clients identify where they are in the grief process and what further steps they need to take in order to move on.

Truck wash

Materials needed

A quantity of large (garbage pail-size) plastic sacks, green or black, depending on preference. Pairs of strong scissors. Possibly lively music and a media player.

Instructions

The facilitator explains to clients that they are going to make some soft brushes for a truck wash. Explain that a large truck going down a busy motorway or main road is likely to pick up plenty of dirt, dust and road slush. This all needs cleaning off regularly so that the truck looks good and doesn't start to deteriorate and get rusty. In a similar way, the stress of life leaves people feeling contaminated. *Truck Wash* can help to 'wash away' leaving the client refreshed and invigorated.

Start by making the soft brushes for the truck wash. Tie a good sized knot in the bottom (sealed) end of each plastic bag. One person holds the knot while the other cuts long strips from the open end right up until nearly to the knot. This is best achieved with the bag held taut. Once the strips are cut, separate them out as much as possible to form a kind of pompom soft brush.

Once everyone has two brushes, practice brushing movements individually for a few minutes. Then get people to take it in turns to stand in the middle of the room with the other/s gently brushing the 'truck' clean, from head (roof) to foot (underside) and back again several times. Make sure every area of the truck is gently cleaned. This can be done using lively music. Some clients will want to enter the truck wash again and again.

Caution: Ensure that clients brush others gently. There is a great temptation for the boys to use the brushes as beaters, which can sting badly.

Objectives

This activity, adapted by us for work with clients, is based on the Car Wash developed by Marie Ware for movement in play therapy (Ware, 2005). It is highly effective for giving and receiving positive messages through gentle contact with the body. It is an excellent activity for building self-esteem and developing confidence. Clients who have been abused may at first find the swishing movements of the brushes a bit frightened but hopefully, if they can come through their initial reaction, they will soon enjoy safe contact with others. *Truck Wash,* because of its pleasant, gentle effect on the body, may well be requested by clients again and again.

Look into my eyes

Materials needed

None.

Instructions

Look into My Eyes is a familiar game in which two people stare each other in the eye from as short a distance as they dare and for as long as possible.

In working with an individual client or a group, the rules can vary. One approach could be to see which of the two laughs first. This usually results in both competitors, as well as any observers, laughing. Another activity involves one person being serious and frowning, and the other person trying his or her best to get the person to laugh, smile or change to a lighter-hearted attitude.

A final activity, if there is time, is what Dr Eric Berne called the 'intimacy experiment' (Berne, 1964). Two people stare into each other's eyes from a distance of approximately 20 inches (50 cm) and see how long they can maintain eye contact. After several minutes, people may experience feelings of closeness in ways that they may not have experienced since they were babies.

Remember that if you are working with clients who have attachment difficulties or problems on the autistic spectrum they will find it difficult if not impossible to look someone direct in they eyes.

Objectives

Look into My Eyes is not only enjoyable. It recreates an experience that children (and adults) rarely if ever experience in their conscious memory. Looking closely into someone's eyes can help build a sense of self-esteem and genuine importance that may be missing. Focusing completely on another person may, through body awareness, take that person back to babyhood, when staring into mother's (or another primary carer's) eyes was the main way of contacting the world.

Take care and protect yourself

Materials needed

None.

Instructions

The focus of this activity is anxiety and its close partner panic.

Start by discussing with clients steps they can take to take care of and protect themselves. This will minimise their need for anxiety and scare. Possible subject areas for discussion could include:

❒ Locking doors and windows at night.
❒ Avoiding danger areas such as dark alleys.
❒ Carrying a screech alarm.
❒ Being cautious about disclosing personal details on the internet.

Next, explore with them symptoms of anxiety/panic that people could experience in their bodies, such as:

❒ Heart racing.
❒ Tight chest.
❒ Stomach turning over.
❒ Hands shaking.

Encourage clients to come up with ideas for dealing with such scary symptoms, such as:

❒ Being aware of their needs.
❒ Calming drink at bedtime.
❒ Avoiding scary movies late at night.

Finally, invite your clients to make a series of body sculptures, by holding their body in a certain position. These could show anxiety and then relaxation, panic and then calmness.

Objectives

No human being is immune from anxiety. It is an essential emotion that gives people the strength and ability to survive and get their needs met. When people experience anxiety for no particular reason, it can hinder them in their lives. *Take Care and Protect Yourself* brings into clients' awareness the importance of anticipating scare, anxiety and panic. Awareness can result in taking steps to avoid as much as possible situations that could heighten anxiety. The body sculptures can enable clients to use bodywork to change their attitudes to anxiety.

Laugh and be happy

Materials needed

None.

Instructions

Laughter is an important ingredient in therapy. With you, clients can let go of themselves and enjoy uncensored laughter. Discuss with clients happiness and laughter.

❐ What does happiness look like?
❐ Where in your body do you feel happiness?
❐ How would you like to express happiness?
❐ If you were happy how would others notice?

Ask your clients to show happiness with their body, such as smiling, laughing, moving. Propose an imaginary toast to your client's happiness. Try laughing together.

Get clients to be aware of their breathing, and bodily sense of well-being as you experience happiness together.

Objectives

The emotion of happiness may be out of clients' recent experience. *Laugh and Be Happy* can help clients to experience the emotion of happiness and learn to express their feelings of happiness in a safe and appropriate way. Laughter releases endorphins that are good for the body and mind.

Enda Junkins writes in connection with therapy: 'We need to laugh more and seek stress-reducing humour in our everyday lives. Laughter is the human gift for coping and for survival. Laughter ringing, laughter pealing, laughter roaring, laughter bubbling. Chuckling. Giggling. Snickering. Snorting. These are the sounds of soul-saving laughter that spring from our emotional core and help us feel better, see things more clearly, and creatively weigh and use our options.

'Laughter helps us roll with the punches that inevitably come our way. The power of laughter is unleashed every time we laugh. In today's stressful world, we need to laugh much more' (Junkins, 2008).

Stay in control

Materials needed

None.

Instructions

Stay in Control consists of a series of enjoyable ways to control aspects of the body. These instructions refer to groups. If you are working with an individual client, adapt them to suit your client's needs.

Everyone lies face down on the floor with arms by sides. The facilitator says: 'Now!' and everyone arches their backs, lifting their head and legs off the floor, leaving only the middle part of their body touching. They hold for as long as they can. An average time for the whole group is worked out and the group then try it again, attempting to increase or reduce the average time.

Everyone turns on their backs and at a given signal they count the number of breaths each person takes. Again, the group finds the average breaths for 10 seconds. Then they try to breathe 10 times in 10 seconds, followed by once in 10 seconds. The facilitator needs to count the seconds off in order to make this effective.

Standing up, the group members walk quickly across the room, counting the number of steps they take in a given time. Then they attempt the same thing slowing down to one step every five seconds.

Finally, they stand still and sway back and forth as far as they can go without falling over. Perhaps you can encourage them to have a competition to see who can sway the furthest without falling over.

Objectives

Stay in Control is a bodywork activity that helps clients to focus on controlling their bodies and (for groups) working together to learn control. By learning to control their bodies clients will also hopefully start to learn how to deal with other 'out of control' body functions they might have such as panic, depression or involuntary tics.

Peace movement

Materials needed

Various tracks of peaceful music from different artistes. A media player.

Instructions

Explore with clients how they can get some peace in their lives. Tell them you are going to play several tracks of peaceful music and invite them to choose one that they will dance or move to.

Ask them to sit comfortably, relax and close their eyes if they would like. Play the pieces of music or extracts from them. Sit silently while clients listen. When the music is finished ask clients to come back into the here and now when they are ready. It is important not to rush them.

Invite clients to choose which piece of music they would like to move their body to. Play the track they have chosen and watch respectfully as they dance or move to the music.

When the music has finished ask them how they found the experience and how it was different from merely listening to the music. It might be useful for you as the therapist to give positive comments on your observation of the dance/movement. For example: 'You seemed peaceful when you did that,' or: 'Your face looked relaxed.'

Objectives

This activity can help clients to find a place in themselves where they can feel peaceful despite what is happening around them. The track of music they have chosen could be used at home as a significant anchor to peace.

Body self-care

Introduction

We live in an increasingly violent society. Clients need to become aware of their weak spots and ways of protecting themselves from aggressors and abusers. Such clients will be more healthy and confident than those who are poorly self-aware and who leave themselves vulnerable to bullying, intimidation and abuse.

Conversely, some clients are themselves aggressors or bullies. They are not aware of their own strength or the negative effect they are having on others. They too need to learn 'body self-care'.

Survival expert Ken Griffiths emphasises the importance of finding the aggressor's social conscience and communicating with him/her to diffuse a potentially violent situation. He writes: 'If we show a lack of confidence, we give the aggressor a signal of our uncertainty and vulnerability. Once this happens, any remaining negotiation is one-sided – his side! If we can continue to show confidence, we can often avoid physical confrontation' (Griffiths, 2002, page 10).

Being confident and self-aware will help clients stay grounded and spatially aware, defend themselves and even say no without smiling.

Self-defence

Materials needed

Toy gun, rolled up newspaper or an empty two-litre plastic bottle to represent a cosh.

Instructions

Self-defence is a way of surviving when all else has failed. It is important that you as the facilitator explain to clients that it is only used as a last resort when their bodies, families or even lives are being threatened. If an aggressor tries to take their bag/wallet or their smart phone, it is far better to let the aggressor have the item than for clients to risk their life trying to keep it.

The following activities are designed for group use and can work just as well with you and your individual client.

The first step to self-defence is for clients to be aware of others when they walk through the car park, down the street or in the local park. When they are near other people they don't know, they need to expect the unexpected and plan an escape route in case there is trouble.

Escape route. This can be practiced as a role-play, with the weakest member of the group being the bully and the most aggressive person finding out what it is like to be the vulnerable one. Then discuss together about the experience afterwards.

Stand your ground. If clients are under attack and can't run away, they can protect themselves physically by the way they stand. Get group members to stand in the protective position: turn body so left shoulder faces attacker. Keep feet firmly on ground, left foot pointing to attacker, with knee bent slightly. Move right foot back with leg straight to stabilise body. Tuck chin down and keep mouth closed. Protect exposed side of face with right hand and use left hand to protect groin area. Lean back so head is out of the way.

There are hundreds of different forms of self-defence ranging from Judo and Jujitsu to Tae Kwan Do and Karate. It is likely in any group of young people that there is at least one who has attended training in some form of martial art or self-defence. Talk together about these, bearing in mind that practicing these without an expert present could result in serious injury or even death.

There are three enjoyable activities you can do with clients to enable them to think about self-defence.

Shoulder touching. In pairs, get clients to attempt to touch each other's shoulders using either hand. Clients also need to protect their own shoulders. This is done by blocking (using the blade of the arm to push away the partner's arm). This activity is great when clients (and therapists!) can move really fast.

Bottle attack. A second activity involves a role play with one person 'attacking' with a raised empty plastic bottle or rolled-up newspaper in his (or her) right hand. The defender grabs the right wrist with his left hand. He puts his right hand under the attacker's arm, brings it to the front and grasps his own left arm, then pushes very gently. *Severe warning: If the attacker in this role play does not fall on the floor his arm will* **definitely** *be broken.*

Hands up! A third activity involves someone pointing a toy gun at close range. The person says: 'Put your hands up!' The idea is to obey the instruction, but as the hands go up, hit the gunman's wrist with one hand, turning to one side so there is less of a target to hit. Then, with the other hand, twist the gun out of the intruder's hand. Mention to clients that if someone ever pointed a gun at them it is unlikely that they will be near enough to defend themselves in this way.

Objectives

Clients who are aware of potential danger and know how to protect themselves, even in very small ways, will be much more confident in themselves. Their sense of self-esteem will increase and the possibility of being bullied or intimidated will be reduced. The client who tends to bully or intimidate others will hopefully learn what it is like for those he/she hurts. This can help such clients to make better choices in the future.

Grounding skills

Materials needed

Can of cold drink. Mints or hard sweets. Handheld mirror.

Instructions

Grounding skills can be done when the client is alone or with another person. If you are working with a group, get them into pairs and each partner take turns in helping the other person to practise becoming grounded in the present.

Aware of senses. One way of grounding is through the senses: *Look* around the room, noticing details. *Touch* or hold a coin, keys or smart phone. Put a cold can of drink against your cheek. *Listen* to your favourite music. What can you *smell* right now? Find a mint or other sweet and *taste* it as if for the first time. *Make contact* by putting your feet solidly of the floor. *Focus* on someone else's voice.

Thinking skills. Ask questions and give answers: Where am I? What's the date? How old am I? What season is it? What is three times eight [or nine times seven]? When is my friend's birthday?

Practical ideas. Breathe deeply and slowly. Look in the mirror and talk to yourself. Pray. Punch some pillows to get rid of anger. Do a drawing. Do five press-ups or run on the spot for 30 seconds.

Objectives

Grounding Skills is an approach that enables clients to stay in the present moment when they are overwhelmed with intense and uncontrollable emotions such as anxiety, panic, fear, shame, guilt or confusion. They are especially useful for clients who dissociate or have sudden flashbacks because of past or present trauma, including abuse. Learning grounding skills is good practice for everyone.

Spatial awareness

Materials needed

None.

Instructions

These instructions assume you are working with a group. They can, of course, be adapted if you are working with an individual.

In pairs stand one each side of the room. Take one step forward, stop and consider whether the distance feels comfortable. Continue until either person feels uncomfortable. Then both people take one step forward to experience discomfort and quickly back away until they reach a point of mutual comfort.

Now try the same exercise, each person holding a cup or glass as if they were having a drink. The cup/glass and the position of the arm form a barrier and usually result in less discomfort.

Sit facing each other and move chairs closer until discomfort is felt. Then put something between the chairs, such as a coffee table, and see if that makes it easier to move closer.

Finally, put two chairs or several chairs side by side. Sit down, all facing forward (as if watching TV or a film at the cinema). Discuss why it is possible to sit so close without feeling invaded. (Examples could include: Eyes facing forward; not looking directly at each other; closeness without threat.)

Objectives

This exercise helps clients to learn about their own personal space. People whose space has been repeatedly invaded may have lost their ability to recognise when it is happening. A small child who has been repeatedly threatened by a shouting adult centimetres from the child's face may end up later in life invading other people's space without realising it.

What Wilson and Ryan (1992/2005) wrote about therapy with children could equally apply with adult clients: 'The physical distance between therapists and children always merits consideration. This is particularly true for abused children and adolescents. They have already experienced an intrusion on their person space, their privacy and perhaps their bodies, by their abusers. In nondirective therapy children maintain control over the distance between themselves and their therapists. . . This stance is part of communicating a sense of safety and predictability for all children in play therapy. With those who have been maltreated, and in various ways have had their own physical as well as psychological boundaries intruded upon, it is understandably even more important' (page 255).

This exercise is useful for all clients, especially those who have been abused, bullied or threatened.

Caring for me

Materials needed

Handcream suitable for your clients.

Instructions

Explore with clients their uniqueness. Look at fingerprints and talk about the patterns in their iris (the coloured part of the eye). Encourage clients to take care of themselves and their bodies, seeing this as something positive and useful for their therapeutic journey.

Take some handcream and, with your client's permission, massage it into each other's hands. This can become something playful, doing high fives and handshakes while rubbing the cream in. Use firm action when massaging each other's hand to avoid 'sensual' touching. *WARNING: Some people may be allergic to lanolin or other ingredients in the handcream so it is essential to check before starting this exercise.*

Discuss about getting enough sleep, eating properly and drinking enough fluid. Talk about taking exercise that suits their lifestyle and that they enjoy. Remind them to make time for relaxation and fun.

Objectives

The aim of this exercise is to help clients value themselves, see themselves as unique and invest the time into caring for themselves. This will enable clients to make any lifestyle changes that are necessary.

Saying no

Materials needed

A handheld mirror.

Instructions

People sometimes find it difficult to say no and be taken seriously. Discuss with your clients about incongruency between what they say and their facial expressions. For example, if clients say no while smiling, people will assume that they are saying yes.

Use a mirror for clients to practise saying no firmly without being aggressive. Get clients to look in the mirror and say no without smiling. Practice using the mirror and make any adjustments necessary. Sometimes clients will say no without smiling and at the very last moment the corners of their mouth turn up. Invite them to hold the pose in the same a singer does at the end of the song.

Now consider together clients' tone of voice. If the voice goes higher at the end, it may be an indication that the 'No' is not serious, perhaps even jokey or questioning. If the voice is very soft, this could be seen as clients doubting themselves.

It is important that these exercises are practiced regularly in front of a mirror between sessions until clients can say no in a convincing, natural way in the session.

Objectives

This skill will hopefully increase clients' self-confidence as other people begin to take them seriously. It can help clients to put boundaries in place and reduce the risk of bullying and intimidation. In the case of child clients it could help to prevent further bullying and abuse.

Strategies for sleep

Materials needed

Relaxing music. A media player.

Instructions

While talking about strategies for sleep, play some gentle, relaxing music to put clients in a relaxed mood. Discuss the importance of getting enough rest and sleep. Sleep gives us the energy to face another day. It enables us to be more tolerant in stressful situations.

Strong sleeping tablets or alcohol just before bedtime can lead to dependency. Suggest instead that clients have a warm bath and a milky drink before going to bed. Certain drinks (such as Horlicks) have natural ingredients to encourage sleep. These are the same ingredients that are used in natural sleep remedies available at healthfood shops and some pharmacies. These could be considered as an alternative to prescribed sleeping products.

Clients could also listen to gentle, soothing music that, if they want, they can continue with in bed using an MP3 player. If they have trouble staying asleep, suggest they keep a notebook by their bed to write down worries and plans so that they clear their mind. They may also want to listen to some more music.

When people are staying awake for long periods of time it can cause a lot of stress. Reassure clients that their bodies will get the rest they need. If clients lie awake they might consider getting up and reading something that is boring or uninteresting. They could also do something to take their minds off 'not sleeping'. They could stare out of the window into the darkness, do the ironing or tidy up. Soon they will find themselves wanting to sleep.

Objectives

Strategies for Sleep can help clients to improve their sleep patterns and get into a good routine of rest and relaxation.

Winning formula

Materials needed

Two large triangles. Put a word in each corner of the Drama Triangle: Victim, Persecutor, Rescuer. For the Winner's Triangle the corners are: Vulnerable, Assertive, Caring.

Instructions

When people interact they often get into what are known as psychological games that end up with both people feeling bad. Stephen Karpman (1968) identified what he called the Drama Triangle. This explains how bullying and intimidation so often becomes a part of a person's life.

Look with your clients at the three positions on the simplified Drama Triangle. The **Victim** acts as if he or she does not have the resources to solve the problem. The **Rescuer** takes over the Victim's thinking and problem-solving. The **Persecutor** acts in his or her own interests and others suffer as a result. The roles can be switched at any point so that a Rescuer can end up as a Victim, or a Persecutor can become a Rescuer.

Invite clients to stand in each of three corners in turn. Ask at each point how the client is thinking, feeling and behaving. How might being on the Drama Triangle help or hinder dealing with bullying or intimidation?

Now look together at the Winner's Triangle (Choy, 1990). The **Vulnerable** person is self-aware and uses his or her skill and thinking for problem-solving. The **Caring** person uses listening skills and self-awareness rather than taking over the Victim's problems. The **Assertive** person asks for what he or she wants and initiates negotiation. Again, the roles can be switched either way.

Invite your client to move to the three corners in turn and say what is their feeling, thinking and behaviour. How might being on the Winner's Triangle help or hinder dealing with bullying or intimidation?

Objectives

Winning Formula is intended to help clients who are susceptible to bullying and intimidation by others. It gives strategies for making changes in attitude and approach so that the Victim can become Vulnerable leading to the Assertive role. By changing formulae, clients can change for the better their role in relationships.

One good thing

Materials needed

None.

Instructions

In order for clients to be more successful in life they need to have confidence in themselves. One way of helping them is by exploring their strengths and positive qualities. Clients are invited to write these down and for each one they show by moving their body this positive attribute. Examples could include: Skilled cook; organiser; safe driver; caring pet owner; good parent; loving friend. Clients may need help to find the positive qualities. The therapist may suggest things he or she has noticed such as being on time, taking care of their appearance or being friendly.

Another way to help clients have confidence in themselves is by their highlighting one aspect of their body that they are proud of. Examples could include nice hair, strong muscles, good skin, attractive face and being happy with their height. Clients who struggle with this could be prompted to use metaphors such as caring hands, a loving heart and an active brain. Once the quality is identified, clients use their bodies to demonstrate this positive aspect of themselves.

Objectives

This activity promotes confidence and self-esteem. Clients who feel good about themselves are better skilled at self-care, including changing therapeutically. They can also take care of others and have a more positive outlook on life. Young teenagers with low self-esteem would benefit particularly from finding *One Good Thing* about themselves.

Sources and references

Baxter, Kate, et al (1994). *Fundamental Activities Handbook*. Nottingham: Fundamental Activities.

Berne, Eric (1964). Social dynamics: The intimacy experiment. *Transactional Analysis Journal, 064,* 09, page 113.

Berne, Eric (1975). *What do you say after you say hello?* London: Corgi. (Original work published 1972.)

Brandes, Donna, & Phillips, Howard (1978). *Gamesters' Handbook: 140 games for teachers and group leaders.* London: Hutchinson. (Original work published 1977.)

Choy, Acey (1990). The winner's triangle. *Transactional Analysis Journal, 20,* 1, pages 40-46.

Davis, Jim (2004). In the shadow of the hug. ITA Conference workshop presentation, 16 April 2004.

Drost, Joost, & Bailey, Sydney (2001). *Therapeutic Groupwork with Children.* Bicester: Speechmark.

Gladwell, Malcolm (2006). *Blink: The power of thinking without thinking.* London: Penguin.

Griffiths, Ken (2002). *The Survival Manual.* London: Carlton Books.

Hasler, Joy (2005). Workshop presentation, 10 June 2005. Fairwarp, Uckfield.

Jennings, Sue (1986). *Creative Drama in Groupwork.* Bicester; Speechmark.

Junkins, Enda (2008). Worldwide web. www.laughertherapy.com

Karpman, Stephen (1968). Fairy tales and script drama analysis. *Transactional Analysis Bulletin, 7,* 26, pages 39-43.

Kranowitz, Carol Stock (2003). *The Out-of-Sync Child Has Fun,* New York: Perigee, 2004.

Kranowitcz, Carol Stock (2005). *The Out-of-Syn Child: Recognising and coping with Sensory Process Disorder.* London: Penguin/Skylight Press. (Original work published 1998.)

Kübler-Ross, E (1969). *On Death and Dying.* New York : Macmillan.

Leben, Norma (1993-1999*). Directive Group Play Therapy: 60 structured games for the treatment of ADHD, low self-esteem and traumatised children.* Pflugerville, Texas: Morning Glory Treatment Center for Children.

McMahon, Linnet (1992). *The Handbook of Play Therapy.* London: Routledge.

Nicholls, Andrews, et al (1992). *Stress Check.* Beoley, Worcestershire: Berean Projects Ltd

Play for Life (2005). 'Canmore 2005 conference report – Attachment theory – The role of fathers'. Play Therapy International: *Play for Life,* Winter 2005, pages 21-4.

Stewart, Ian, & Joines, Vann (1987). *TA Today: A new introduction to Transactional Analysis.* Nottingham: Lifespace Publishing.

Vizard, Eileen (1986). *Self-esteem and Personal Safety: A guide for professionals working with sexually abused children.* London: The Great Ormond Street Hospital Child Sexual Abuse Treatment Programme, Tavistock Publications.

Ware, Marie (2004). Speaking notes, Play Therapy World Congress, Chichester.

Ware, Marie (2005). Workshop presentation, Fairwarp, Uckfield. 22 January 2005

White, Tony. Symbiosis and attachment hunger. *Transactional Analysis Journal, 27,* 4, 1997.

Whitehouse, Éliane, & Pudney, Warwick (1996). *A Volcano in My Tummy: Helping children to handle anger.* Gabriola Island, British Columbia: New Society Publishers.

Wilson, Kate, & Ryan, Virginia (2005). *Play Therapy: A nondirective approach for children and adolescents,* Kate Wilson & Virginia Ryan, London: Baillière Tindall. (Original work published 1992.)

Printed in Great Britain
by Amazon